...And the
Diamonds
Were Taken...

Female Genital Mutilation and
Its Global Ramifications

...And the

Diamonds

Were Taken...

Female Genital Mutilation and
Its Global Ramifications

O. Mark Eda

MBA, MSC, BSC Bus Admin, DIP Journalism

iUniverse

...And the Diamonds Were Taken...
Female Genital Mutilation and Its Global Ramifications

AMP
Scripture quotations marked AMP are from The Amplified Bible, Old Testament copyright © 1965, 1987 by the Zondervan Corporation. The Amplified Bible, New Testament copyright © 1954, 1958, 1987 by The Lockman Foundation. Used by permission. All rights reserved.

KJV
Scripture quotations marked KJV are from the Holy Bible, King James Version (Authorized Version). First published in 1611. Quoted from the KJV Classic Reference Bible, Copyright © 1983 by The Zondervan Corporation.

ESV
Unless otherwise indicated, all scripture quotations are from The Holy Bible, English Standard Version® (ESV®). Copyright ©2001 by Crossway Bibles, a division of Good News Publishers. Used by permission. All rights reserved.

iUniverse books may be ordered through booksellers or by contacting:

iUniverse
1663 Liberty Drive
Bloomington, IN 47403
www.iuniverse.com
1-800-Authors (1-800-288-4677)

Because of the dynamic nature of the Internet, any web addresses or links contained in this book may have changed since publication and may no longer be valid. The views expressed in this work are solely those of the author and do not necessarily reflect the views of the publisher, and the publisher hereby disclaims any responsibility for them.

Any people depicted in stock imagery provided by Getty Images are models, and such images are being used for illustrative purposes only.

Certain stock imagery © Getty Images.

ISBN: 978-1-5320-8673-1 (sc)
ISBN: 978-1-5320-8674-8 (hc)
ISBN: 978-1-5320-8672-4 (e)

Library of Congress Control Number: 2019917175

Print information available on the last page.

iUniverse rev. date: 10/30/2019

Contents

Preface

C ircumcision is an ancient custom around the world. Even in countries like Egypt, in considering the genesis of this concern, leaders still seem puzzled about what to do differently if given access to other choices. In the early years of circumcision, the concept was linked only to males, and it was not until later years that females were brought into the equation. The health concerns expressed by practicing communities have been jaw-dropping.

The controversies surrounding female genital mutilation (FGM) around the world are so great that ignoring them, not doing them proper justice in the area of enlightenment and education concerning the entire premise, would be improper. My journey around the globe to put the concept of FGM in perspective, in some cases, may have been personal, but it has also been one of my best fact-finding ventures.

With some individuals appearing on Oprah Winfrey's talk show and other well-watched shows around the United States of

America (USA), in some cases, stories are being told and usually not in their entirety. The need for a somewhat complete story with a better understanding and comprehension of the subject matter has constantly been on my mind to the extent that I thought writing *And the Diamonds Were Taken* might be all I need to do to accomplish my desired goal with regard to FGM.

Though the World Health Organization (WHO), the United Nations Children's Fund (originally known as the United Nations International Children's Emergency Fund [UNICEF]), and many other organizations in communities around the world may appear relentless in their fight against this heinous practice, its total elimination may be impossible. However, the tenacity of the laws governing FGM around the world may come to bear in actually discouraging the individuals involved, leading to a reduction of the practice of this ancient custom as it is known today.

I strongly believe that men in the practicing communities around the world should be engaged and included in the decision-making, as it has been seen as means of control over women in some reports in certain quarters around these communities.

The Trip to West Africa

The weather on this fateful day was unusual, as the summer heat was so overbearing. Anyone in their right mind would think twice before attempting to explore the outdoors. For some reason, this was the day that Mr. Jones and his daughter, Cindy, chose to travel. The usually crowded Los Angeles International Airport (LAX) appeared to have unusually light traffic. This could have been blamed on the bad weather, as a result of which check-in time was faster than normal.

Patience was running out for every passenger awaiting the 4:50p.m. Lufthansa flight from Frankfurt, Germany, which was about an hour late because of bad weather, which caused turbulence throughout the ten-hour flight.

On arrival, Flight 712 was expected to stop for about an hour in Frankfurt for a connecting flight to Nigeria, West Africa. It was at the waiting area in LAX that curious Cindy spotted a family sitting not too far from them. She could hear them speaking a Nigerian

1

dialect. She did not waste any time before approaching them. Upon getting to them, after exchanging pleasantries and greetings with the family, she looked straight in the direction of the elderly lady in the group, Mrs. Okoro, and asked her if females were actually circumcised. It was true, that up until this moment, she had not believed it, and this reality continued to remain in her mind as a mere concept. The latter brought about long historical references and supposed facts and fallacies regarding both male and female circumcision and their importance to the various communities that practiced it around the world.

Just as expected, the meeting with the Okoro family further increased Cindy's curiosity, and she became even more impatient while anticipating her first experience of this exercise or actual performance of circumcision on a person. By the time Cindy returned to her seat in the waiting area, the boarding announcement had just begun.

A Portrait of A Typical Village Home On A Beautiful Evening

The nearly ten-hour flight from Frankfurt to Lagos, Nigeria, was troubled by several instances of turbulence due to bad weather. But the flight captain was poised to make the flight as smooth as possible. As announcement followed by announcement permeated much of the flight, most passengers could not fall asleep. After the turbulence resolved, the calm passengers experienced for the remaining two hours to Lagos was unprecedented—until they felt the sudden jerks preceding the announcement from the flight deck.

A feminine-sounding voice said, "Fasten your seatbelts, as we're about to make our descent into Murtala Muhammed International Airport. We are about to land." As the pilot started descending, in preparation to land, most of the passengers on board suddenly woke up, with the exception of those with their ears plugged listening to music. Out of curiosity, some of the passengers by the window looked out and were welcomed by the unending rusted-iron roofs and other scenes on the ground.

The episode was short-lived. Passengers could hear the sudden sound of the landing gears and wheels being released; at the same time, the engine slowed down as the wheels touched the runway.

"We will be arriving in approximately ten minutes. Please fasten your seat belts and make sure your trays are clear and in an upright position. Please do not leave your seats until we are safely in the boarding zone. Thank you for flying Victory Airlines."

He studied the woman's face for a moment. She looked to be in her forties and very nervous. Her eyes seemed to roam around the cabin as if she were expecting something to happen. A young boy who was probably her son sat next to her with wide eyes as he studied the skies. He looked to be the same age as his kid sister. The woman's hands trembled as she checked his seat belt. Beside him, his ten-year-old sister was still listening to her favorite music, not caring or even aware that the airplane was about to touch down.

Flight 712 appeared to be tilting slightly to the left and began a slow and steady turn. Down below, the ground looked like square plots on a huge map of some kind. Gradually, everything came into view. As they neared the ground, small cars heading down long highways of black ribbon appeared, as well as various homes of different sizes, colors, and shapes. A sudden bump told him the landing gear had been released. The woman jumped slightly at the sound.

Feeling his ears pop, he opened his mouth in an attempt to release the pressure. Trees and rooftops whizzed by in a flash as the aircraft made its final turn onto the waiting runway with a mild rumbling as the tires kissed the tarmac. A loud rush of air giving pressure to the brakes slowly brought the plane to an Indy 500 speed, culminating in the final act of taxiing slowly but surely into the arrival gate.

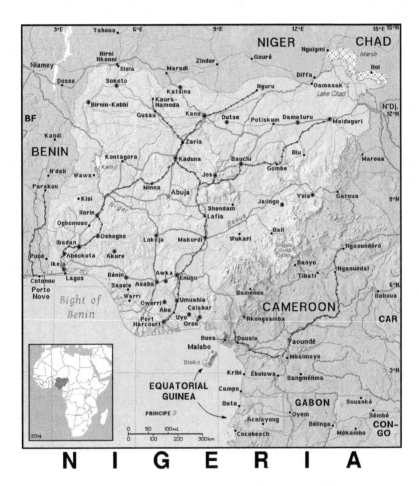

N I G E R I A

Culture and Its Diversities

H istorically, every community around the globe has been endowed with cultural differences. Some are jaw-dropping and may sometimes sound like something from outer space. The importance of cultures in our communities around the world cannot be overemphasized, as living without them may be likened to not being in existence. Just like the cliché says, we are who we are based on our cultural backgrounds and the continued struggle in attempting to fit perfectly into whatever communities we may find ourselves residing in. The latter seems to be a lifetime struggle in every ethnicity, as we all find ourselves at birth boarding that train they say goes nowhere, and we are all passengers on this train, awaiting exit in due time.

Although most definitions of ethics appear to focus on human behaviors as they relate to what is good and bad or what is moral and immoral, humans' ability to effectively use these concepts in their day-to-day dealings is still not without some undertones. Realistically speaking, ethical reasoning seems to transcend beyond those boundaries.

The Webster's II New Riverside University Dictionary's definition of *ethics* describes ethics as a set of moral principles or values such that should be followed by professional individuals, organizations, and so on. *Ethical* is defined as "of or relating to ethics, conforming to accepted professional standards of conduct."

What appears to make the issue of ethics more relative is the fact that humans are very unique and different from one another; because of the diverse nature of humans, it becomes very important for everyone to be able to live side by side with one another, whether in a social setting or work environment, without problems that may have otherwise surfaced because of the differences in our various qualities.

By the same token, ethical reasoning without a proper understanding and comprehension of the cultural differences of others may never be a reality. In all facets of today's existence, recognizing that people from different cultural backgrounds might bring different sets of experiences and skills into their relationships, workplaces, and homes does not particularly dictate a cultural-identity-based division of labor among the people.

To be ethically effective, a community must stay in touch with what today's culture expects and does not necessarily have to be doing what is right in the eyes of all. We should all consider ethical conduct in communities as standards intended to keep people's behavior under control but not because they are as good as the results they achieve. In my mind, a society is viewed as being ethical when its basic principles seem fair to everyone who examines them. Humans should consider a policy ethical only when basic values are considered and included in its definition, and not in only the light of the benefits to us individually or the society outweighing the costs.

In the same vein, to be ethically effective, an individual must stay in touch with what today's culture expects and does not necessarily have to perform good works.

In my mind, a person is viewed as being ethical when his or her basic principles seem fair to everyone who examines them. He or she may not be someone who considers persons and communities as being of prime importance. Humans should consider a policy ethical only when basic values are considered and included in its definition.

Local Community Members Seen Involved In
Their Various Activities On A Typical Day

Culture comes in various varieties and flavors. In Venezuela, a young woman's coming out or introduction to society is performed by going on the top of a mountain, whereas in Hispanic culture, a young woman's coming to maturity is determined when she turns fifteen years old. The latter is usually followed by a lavishly expensive party given by her parents.

Just like anything in life, this exercise of male circumcision has been wrapped in serious health situations that appear to have their ups and downs, especially in the medical environment or parlance. In terms of medical ramifications for this exercise, Google stated the following: "It is known that there is evidence that circumcision has health benefits, including a decreased risk of urinary tract infections and a reduced risk of some sexually transmitted diseases. Of these concerns, protection against penile cancer and a reduced risk of cervical cancer in female sex partners seemed to top the list".

And, with regard to women, there is also a belief that infibulation of the vulva increases hygiene. The common reasons for FGM cited by women in surveys are the following: social acceptance, religion, hygiene, preservation of virginity, marriage eligibility, and enhancement of male sexual pleasure. However, reports that circumcision could help prevent penile infection, penile cancer, and cervical cancer in partners of men still remain unfounded, as there has not been any report positively supporting this belief.

In a study by L. A. Briggs of the Department of Human Kinetics, Health and Safety Education, Rivers State College of Education in Port Harcourt, Nigeria, on "Male and Female Viewpoints on Female Circumcision in Ekpeye Region of the State,"195 male and female volunteers across the social strata were interviewed using a structured questionnaire. Data were analyzed using frequency tables. The study revealed that 74.7 percent of female respondents were circumcised.

They believed that the practice would help prevent sexual promiscuity and curb sexual desires and that it was a custom they could not do without. Most of the men would not marry an uncircumcised female, while a substantial number of the respondents wanted to circumcise their daughters. Community efforts to eradicate the practice were very minimal. Based on the findings, the author suggested that communities where FGM is practiced as a social norm should be involved in eradication campaigns with support from national and international organizations.

Happy Cultural Group Dancing During A Market-Day Festival

Another study by J. I. Adinma (1997) of the Department of Obstetrics and Gynecology, Nnamdi Azikiwe Teaching Hospital in Anambra State, Nigeria, titled "Current Status of Female Circumcision among Nigerian Igbos," addressed the issue of FGM, elaborating on the incidence of circumcision in 256 pregnant Nigerian Igbo women with 124 (48.4 percent) being cut. The author, however, observed an increase in this case, attributing the spike to increasing social class (circumcision index [C.I.], 0.06 to 16.50, for social class 1 to 5). It was least prevalent among the youngest age range, sixteen to twenty years (C.I., 0.45), and among the prim gravidae (C.I., 0.36) compared to the grand multipara (C.I., 4.43) ($P < 0.05$). Simple excision was the most common type of circumcision with 122 respondents (98.4 percent). The genital introituses were mildly scarred in 48 respondents (38.7 percent), moderately scarred in 47 (37.9 percent), and severely scarred in 29 (23.4 percent). Up to 36.7 percent of the respondents were not aware of their circumcision status, while 91 (96.8 percent) of the circumcised women had it performed during infancy. On the question of continued practice of female circumcision in their villages, 43 respondents (16.8 percent) replied, "yes"; 138 (53.9 percent), "no"; 25 (9.8 percent), "sometimes"; and 50 (19.5 percent), "don't know." The incidence of episiotomy during delivery was similar for both circumcised respondents, 47 (18.4 percent), and uncircumcised respondents, 46 (18.0 percent) ($P = 0.05$). More uncircumcised respondents, 31 (12.1 percent), were sexually satisfied during intercourse than circumcised, 11 (4.3 percent) ($P < 0.05$). Of the 118 female offspring of the respondents, 109 (92.4 percent) were not circumcised while 9 (7.6 percent) were. Increased public enlightenment on the risks of female circumcision is expected to eradicate the practice by the next generation.

Nigerian family on a typical hot, sunny day

A different study on "Female Circumcision and Determinants in Southern Nigeria," carried out by A.E. Ehigiegba, D.O. Selo-Ojeme, and F.I. Omorogbe of the Department of Obstetrics and Gynecology, University of Benin Teaching Hospital, in Delta State, Nigeria, noted that 192 postnatal women and 95 newly born baby girls were prospectively investigated at the six-week postnatal clinic of the Department of Obstetrics and Gynecology of the University of Benin Teaching Hospital, Benin City, Nigeria, between January 1, 1996, and April 30, 1996. Circumcision was clinically verified in 65 percent of the mothers and in 38 percent of the baby girls. The decision to circumcise the babies was taken in over 90 percent of cases by husbands even though this was opposed by wives in 19 percent of cases. Significantly more circumcised than uncircumcised baby girls had circumcised mothers (P < 0.01), and maternal low educational status was significantly related (P < 0.01) to the tendency to circumcise the babies. There was a lack of antenatal counseling for most mothers. The authors concluded that while the incidence of female circumcision may be declining, attention needs to be focused on proper community enlightenment as well as the role of the male in the decision to circumcise daughters.

Young women in Nigeria dancing during an FGM ceremony

Al Jazeera and agencies in 2014 referenced Jacqueline Badcock, a United Nations representative, who claimed that the Islamic State had issued an order to Mosul women regarding female circumcision, which was later denied by websites linked to the group. The order demanded that females in the Mosul territory of Iraq undergo female circumcision. But the UN's resident humanitarian coordinator's instant intervention led to the rejection of the claim by activists linked to the group.

A group of African ladies on a regular market day

A mother afraid as she protects her child from the unsterilized
knives of female genital mutilation perpetrators in Nigeria

According to Ms. Badcock, at a news conference in Erbil, the decree, which was supposed to affect four million women and girls, was only issued to residents between the ages of eleven and forty-six years who were residing in and around the city of Mosul. The Al Jazeera reporter Omar al Saleh noted that the UN representative described the decree as not being the will of the Iraqi people, especially in the areas covered by the terrorists. The authenticity was, as expected, rejected by Islamic State affiliated websites and Twitter accounts.

In Sierra Leone, female circumcision has a very different dimension because it carries with it a religious connotation, which is also argumentatively implied in most other cultures around the world. But here Muslims are known to practice it primarily to represent their young girls' coming of age. This practice is usually common when these young women are about the age of ten and involves a very lavish and flamboyant ceremony. During this ceremony, whole cows are slaughtered alongside other goodies. The occasion is usually so decorated and beautiful that nonparticipants are envious to the point of wanting to cross over from their various religions and become Muslims.

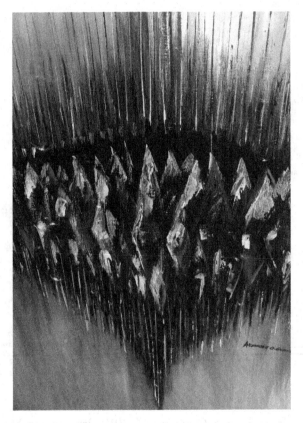

Abstract art depicting a conglomeration of countries
around the world still practicing FGM

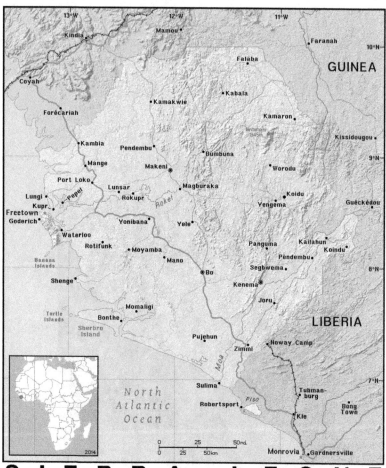

S I E R R A   L E O N E

Credits:

PAT is free software. Copyright © 2010, 2013 by Ian Macky.
PAT maps are public domain.
https://ian.macky.net/pat/license.html

The ceremony would normally take up to three weeks, with every passing day filled with rituals that nonparticipants would always consider to be unbelievable. During the three-week period, the circumcised is usually confined to a single room with only close family members and attending nurses who usually see to the healing of the wounds left by the cutting performed on the young girl. The third week, which is set aside as the coming-out of the young girl is usually used to signify that she's now fully healed and ready for the genesis of her adult life.

African women on a normal day

Today, the type of flamboyant ceremonies that are practiced by the Muslims in Sierra Leone are also known to be happening in other African countries, which makes the Christians continue to distance themselves from this ordeal.

A Northern African lady on a typical day

However, this type of coming-of-age ceremony is also seen being practiced in the Hispanic communities in the United States and around the world, as the parents of these young girls continue throwing lavish parties for their daughters when they turn fifteen years of age. It is common practice after the ceremony that the young girls are considered prepared to be taken for marriage by their peers or older men. In Venezuela, the culture appears to be similar to that seen in Hispanic communities around the world.

An Al Jazeera article by a group of authors on "Do the health benefits of male circumcision outweigh the risks" observed that about 1.1 million Zimbabwean citizens live with HIV, and many studies show that male circumcision could actually reduce the risk of infection by 60 percent. This concern may be looked at differently in the Southern part of the African continent. The report also noted that since 2011, Zimbabwean men and infants have been subjected to involuntary nonsurgical circumcision, against human rights agencies' position on the issue. But, contrary to that country's position on male circumcision, opponents still argue that the risks do not seem to outweigh the benefits and blame this type of information for the false sense of hope regarding HIV prevention.

An African Mother With Her Baby On Her
back On Her Way From The Market

21

A Special Report on 'Female Circumcision: Rite of Passage Or Violation of Rights?' presented by Frances A. Althaus during the 'International Family Planning Perspectives 1997 identified the various types of as follows: "Although circumcision may be performed during infancy, during adolescence or even during a woman's first pregnancy, the procedure is usually carried out on girls between ages four and 12. In the countries for which Demographic and Health Survey (DHS) data are available, the median age at excision ranges from less than two months in Eritrea to about six years in Mali and almost 10 years in Egypt. The operation is generally performed by a traditional birth attendant or an *exciseuse*, an elder village woman".

A young mother and her daughter

According to a publication by the *Mayo Clinic Proceedings*, male circumcision may have been tied to religious and cultural acts for many, but more African men are known to be voluntarily partaking in it for health reasons. The publication also showed how health benefits continue to outweigh the risks of infant circumcision in many countries. Arguing in support of the latter, the World Health Organization discovered that male circumcision has the ability to reduce the risk of heterosexually transmitted HIV infection by 60 percent and encouraged countries like Kenya, Zimbabwe, Uganda, Zambia, Malawi, and South Africa to enforce national circumcision programs.

The Genesis of Female Genital Mutilation

C ircumcision generally has always been known to have emanated from the various traditions and beliefs of communities around the world. These were later accepted as the norms of those communities. It is of importance to also mention the fact that many traditions and customs that these communities have learned must have been left untouched because of civilization as a result of the coming-of-age of these communities.

A presentation by L. B. Moss (1991) at the Second International Symposium on Circumcision in San Francisco, California, "The Jewish Roots of Anti-Circumcision Arguments, "shows how "a carefully considered decision against circumcision can be reconciled within the Jewish tradition." The author started by quoting the following Bible passages from the book of Genesis:

And when Abram was ninety years old and nine, the Lord appeared to Abram, and said unto him, I am the Almighty God; walk in my ways and be blameless. I will establish my covenant between me and you and I will make you exceedingly numerous. And you shall no longer be called Abram, you're your name shall be Abraham and I make you the father of a multitude of nations. I will make you exceedingly fertile and make nations of you and kings shall come forth from you. I will maintain my covenant between me and you to be God to you and your offspring to come. I assign the land you sojourn in to you and your offspring to come, all the land of Canaan, as an everlasting holding; I will be their God. (Genesis: 17: 1-8 AMP)

As for you, you and your offspring to come throughout the ages shall keep my covenant. Such shall be the covenant between me and you and your offspring to follow, which you shall keep: Every male among you shall be circumcised. You shall circumcise the flesh of your foreskin and that shall be the sign of the covenant between me and you. And throughout the generations every male among you shall be circumcised at the age of eight days. Thus shall my covenant be marked in your flesh as an everlasting pact. And if any male who is uncircumcised fails to circumcise the flesh of his foreskin, that person shall be cut off from his skin. He has broken my covenant. (Genesis: 17: 9-14 KJV)

According to Wikipedia, the world's first known campaign against FGM took place in the 1920s in Egypt, in northern Africa. Reports show that FGM prevalence in Egypt in 1995 can be likened to Somalia's 2013 world record of 98 percent. The 2013 UNICEF report covering twenty-nine countries in the continent of Africa and the Middle East had Egypt as topping the region's highest total number of women with a staggering 27.2 million who had experienced the practice (Wikipedia).

An Egyptian chest

According to Gerald Larue (1991), in "Religious Traditions and Circumcision," no records of circumcision of any nature were known before the Egyptian stories regarding male circumcision (BCE). During this time in history, the practice first appeared in the ancient Near East, where exhumed bodies from 4000 BCE in Egypt disclosed evidence of circumcision (Breasted, 10). Larue also argued that male circumcision did not seem to be a mandatory thing, as the practice was not known to be common among men in the local communities. It was the author's belief that this painful mutilation of the foreskins of infant males in America was based on biblical and religious traditions. He believed that "they practice circumcision for the sake of cleanliness, for they place cleanliness before comeliness" (II, 37). "A mythological reference in chapter 17 of the *Egyptian Book of the Dead* states that the sun-god Ra circumcised himself and that from the drops of blood two protective deities came into being, so that perhaps toe was a prophylactic symbolism in the Egyptian practice." The author contends it was proven beyond reasonable doubt that not all Egyptians during this era were circumcised. Larue's research revealed that x-rays of the mummy of the Eighteenth Dynasty Pharaoh Ahomse (sixteenth century BCE) proved that he was not circumcised. There was also the possibility his successor, Amenhotep I, was uncircumcised (Harris and Weeks, 126–130).

A Lady with Her Daughter Strapped To Her
Back on The Way Home From The Farm

It was general belief at this time that circumcision was only common among the upper classes and the affluent and might have been recognized as a puberty rite, but it was never seen as a requirement.

The story about Moses in Exodus stated the following:

> *Then it happened at a stopping place along the way that Yahweh methim [Moses] and tried to kill him. Then Zipporah (Moses's Midianite wife) took a piece of flint and cut off her son's foreskin and touched his feet (genitals) with it, saying, "You are my blood-bridegroom." So he let him alone. At that time she said "blood-bridegroom" in reference to circumcision. (Exodus 4:24–26 AMP)*

The preceding quotation from the Holy Bible was the genesis of what is called circumcision, and it became the Hebrews' custom from the tenth century BCE. According to Larue, the flint-style circumcision, which resulted because of the Hebrews' contact with the Midianites, gave birth to the circumcision of infants. This process is likened to the circumcision before marriage in which a virgin bride would lose her hymen, "testified to by bloody wedding night sheets (Deuteronomy 22:13–19 NIV), which involved the removal of the prepuce becoming the groom's parallel loss." It is of interest how "the circumciser" meant father-in-law in Hebrew. Note also its relationship to premarital circumcision. This era also witnessed the use of a flint blade in place of copper, bronze, and iron, which may touch on the raw nature of the ritual, having to do with the Egyptian custom regarding the use of flint tools when circumcision was carried out.

The other reference of circumcision was in the seventh century BCE when the use of a flint cutting apparatus was seen in the biblical conquest of Palestine story:

> At that time Yahweh said to Joshua, "Make yourself flint knives and squat down and circumcise the people of Israel for a second time." So, Joshua made flint knives and circumcised the people of Israel on the hill of foreskins. (Joshua 5:2–3 ESV)

According to Larue, a still later tradition after the sixth century BCE was traceable to Hebrew circumcision and Abraham. He noted that the deity was able to make a religious-legal covenant with Abraham, who is the father of the Jewish people, making Yahweh the unique god of the Jews whom alone they would worship. Covenants were known to be sealed in ancient times with marks and symbols such as the mark of circumcision:

> For your part you must keep my covenant, you and your descendants … every male among you must be circumcised. You must be circumcised. You shall cut off the flesh of your foreskin, and that will be the symbol of the covenant between us. Throughout all your generations every male shall be circumcised at the age of eight days. (Genesis 17:10–12 AMP)

According the preceding regulation, failure by individuals to be circumcised may result in excommunication, for both Jews and foreigners.

Chapter 4

FGM Compared to Abortion in Other Cultures and HIV

As barbaric as FGM is and considering both the known and unknown voices for and against the idea, comparing this ideology to abortion in other cultures may in some sense mean misrepresentation of these cultures. Of the various movements around the universe, those individuals who are prochoice and otherwise seem overwhelmingly louder in regard to both sides. Comparing circumcision, which does not end or terminate the human's life and abortion, where the decision must be made whether to take a life, considering the arguments in support of and those against the concept, it may be very difficult to draw the line here.

Flipping the coin to the other side, HIV/AIDS is considered a plague when compared to Ebola, cholera, and other diseases, which are always expected to come and go away. Contrary to the latter, HIV and AIDS seem to linger on endlessly, making some scholars look at it as an epidemic that may be here longer than we can ever imagine. According to Wikipedia, the Centers for Disease Control and Prevention (CDC), and the Everyday Health website, an estimated cumulative figure of AIDS cases in the United States is around 1.8 million with about 50,000 new cases of HIV yearly. It is known that some 35.3 million individuals are currently living with HIV/AIDS, and the World Health Organization estimated that 36 million people have died of the virus since the first cases were reported in 1981; 1.6 million died from the disease in 2012 alone.

A Woman On Her Way Home From The Market

I.O. Ogunlola, E.O. Orji, and A.T. Owolabi of the Department of Obstetrics, Gynecology, and Perinatology at the Obafemi

Awolowo University Teaching Hospital Complex, Nigeria, in their article "Female Genital Mutilation and the Unborn Female Child in Southwest Nigeria, "expressed concern over how female genital mutilation is still being widely practiced in Nigeria despite efforts to abolish it. They contended that the risk of FGM to a female child in southwest Nigeria was investigated by interviewing 430 consecutive pregnant women attending the antenatal clinic of Wesley Guild Hospital Ilesha, western Nigeria, between July 2001 and October 2001. The results, according to the authors, show that 60 percent of the pregnant women studied had a type of genital mutilation. The decision to mutilate a female child is taken before she is born. Seventy-four (17.2 percent) of the women and 146 (34 percent) of their husbands would circumcise their female child. Though the decision to circumcise a female child is usually made between the husband and wife, the final decision is believed to come mainly from the husband. Because the majority of the women (58.4 percent) were yet to decide whether or not to circumcise their female children, they could sway the decision either way before the husband made up his mind. Therefore, every effort should be made to involve men in the struggle to eradicate this unwholesome practice.

A typical village lady on her way to the farm

According to the women's center website article on abortion statistics, Orlando Abortion Clinic, one-third of all pregnancies around the world are unplanned, and about 25 percent of the world's population lives in countries with very high and restrictive abortion laws. It is also a fact that one woman dies every seven minutes around the globe because of unsafe illegal pregnancy termination. As a result of these dwindling numbers, it has come to be known that making abortion legal or illegal does not have the propensity to affect these numbers.

A study of female circumcision in Nigeria by O.M. Odujinrin, C.O. Akintoye, and M.A. Oyediran revealed that of the 181 women who were randomly chosen from the women in attendance at a family planning clinic of the Department of Community Health College of Medicine, University of Lagos, from February 1984 to September 1984, 84.7 percent were aged between twenty-five and forty-four, and the Yoruba tribe in western Nigeria was responsible for 70.7 percent of the lot. Though 56.4 percent claimed to have been circumcised, examination revealed that 24.5 percent had no clinical evidence of circumcision. Of the group, the Edo tribe from Edo State had 76.7 percent, which was considered the highest proportion of circumcised individuals among the respondents, with the Ibos at 61 percent, and least of all the Efiks from the middle belt area of the country with 20 percent.

The report from the authors revealed that the majority of the circumcised were infants, making up 78.8 percent of the total, and only 5.9 percent were adults; however, the Ibos from the eastern part of the country and the Yoruba tribe from the west had high rates of infant circumcision. Some of the respondents who were aware of the associated side effects were able to refrain from the exercise. As a result of the latter, it was revealed that the more educated women were less likely to circumcise their daughters. All circumcised daughters were from circumcised mothers except one, and she had to circumcise her daughter in conformity with her husband's tribal practice. Accurate statistics of morbidity and mortality from female circumcision will be difficult to gather, as circumcision is performed mostly in the home; nevertheless, the complications are severe enough to merit authoritative intervention. It is recommended that public awareness of female circumcision, its complications, and other attendant health concerns should be embarked upon by health authorities, especially among the tribes practicing it.

Chapter

5

Countries Supporting FGM and Some Statistics

There are no definitive studies on the prevalence of FGM in Africa and the Middle East. Therefore, it is important to keep in mind that these are only estimates. They are based on Fran Hosken's estimates and date from 1982. In the same year, Ms. Hosken conducted a study that was published as *The Hosken Report*. She estimated that there were more than 79.97 million mutilated females in the world. Today, there are more than 114 million women who have undergone some form of FGM in the world. That's almost double what the 1982 estimates show. The practice of FGM is not only limited to Africa and the Middle East, as stated earlier. Reports show that it is also being practiced in the United States of America.

A portrait of an East African woman
superimposed on an African map

This heinous practice, which was prohibited outright by the Prohibition of Female Circumcision Act 1985 in the United Kingdom, making it an offense to perform this gruesome act on children or adults, is still known to be carried out regardless of the worldwide publicity against it. As recently as 2018, it has been reported that the occurrence of this act is so frequent that one is disturbingly reported every two hours in England.

In a report released in 2019, Bob Cesca (*Salon* 2019) expressed disappointment in the lack of interest from the US government and Attorney General Bill Barr in defending the law against FGM in court to date. The report touched on the half a million girls at risk and exposed to this inhumane practice, according to the CDC, with the lackluster attitude of the US government, especially knowing that the twenty-year ban is about to end.

The author recalled that earlier in 2019, the solicitor general and the third-ranking official of the Department of Justice, Noel Francisco, in view of the excruciating nature of FGM, had sent a correspondence to California Senator Diane Feinstein to give her a heads-up on the Department of Justice's position on this concern. The writer noted that the DOJ's position not to defend the law in court was precipitated by an earlier ruling by a federal judge named Bernard Friedman in the Eastern District of Michigan, who had struck down the law. Cesca contended the judge also stated in his disposition that the FGM ban did not "require interstate activity" to make it legal. Judge Friedman, the author continued, was particularly concerned with the inadequacy of the interstate language to make the federal law valid.

> *The report also stated that the ban of this terrible practice was struck down as part of a case in which a Michigan doctor arranged with the family of two seven-year-old girls from Minnesota to travel to Michigan, where their clitoral hoods were mutilated. The law was used to prosecute the doctor, Jumana Nagarwala, in federal court. But since the interstate aspect of the crime wasn't explicit in the law, Judge Friedman dismissed the charges against the doctor.*

The author expressed distaste in the manner the DOJ has continued to defend the law, losing the battle for a day in the Supreme Court. The report expressed particular concern and dismay over the way America has chosen to give up the fight, resulting in the implied future legalization of FGM in this great country of ours.

The ideology is known to be practiced in thirty countries in western, eastern, and northeastern Africa; parts of the Middle East and Asia; and some immigrant communities in Europe, North America, and Australia. The World Health Organization defines the practice as "all procedures that involve partial or total in some cases removal of the external female genitalia, or other injury to the female genital organs without any medical rational and reasoning" (Wikipedia).

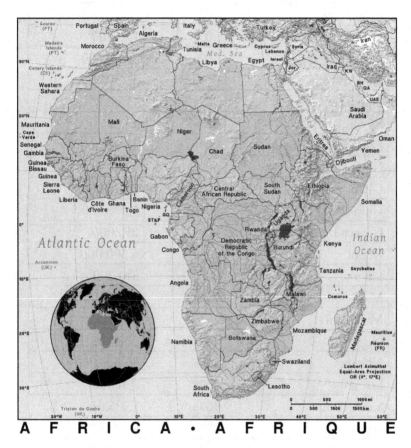

AFRICA · AFRIQUE

Credits:

PAT is free software. Copyright © 2010, 2013 by Ian Macky.

PAT maps are public domain.

https://ian.macky.net/pat/license.html

Country	Prevalence	Actual Number
Benin*	50%	1,200,00
Burkina Faso*	70%	3,290,000
Cameroon*	--	--
Central African Republic*	50%	750,000
Chad	60%	1,530,000
Cote d'Ivoire*	60%	3,750,000
Djibouti	98%	196,000
Egypt	50%	13,625,000
Ethiopia and Eritrea	90%	23,940,000
Gambia*	60%	270,000
Ghana	30%	2,325,000
Guinea*	50%	1,875,000
Guinea Bissau*	50%	250,000
Kenya	50%	6,300,000
Liberia*	60%	810,000
Mali*	75%	3,112,500
Mauritania*	25%	262,500
Niger*	20%	800,000
Nigeria	50%	30,625,000
Senegal	20%	750,000
Sierra Leone	90%	1,935,000
Somalia	98%	3,773,000
Sudan (North)	89%	9,220,400
Tanzania	10%	1,345,000
Togo*	50%	950,000
Uganda*	5%	467,500
Zaire*	5%	945,000
Total		114,296,900

Anecdotal information only; no published studies.

1. Excerpted from Nahid Toubia's *Female Genital Mutilation: A Call for Global Action* (1993).

Nigeria   50%   Clitoridectomy, excision, and, in the northwest, some infibulation FGM is practiced throughout the country and among all ethnic and religious groups. No law specifically prohibits FGM. The National Association of Nigerian Nurses and Midwives (NANNM) has been active in the fight against FGM. Nurses and pediatricians have campaigned throughout the country, conducting educational activities at the state and community levels. In 1984, a Nigerian National Committee, the National Chapter of the IAC, was set up. The committee has had support from the Ministries of Health, Education, and Information.

A Wooden Carving Of A Community Elder

Genital Mutilation and Women's Sexual Sensation

There is nothing in life that does not have a backlash or side effect. These concerns may either be negative or positive, depending on the sector of the community or the person making the assertions. With the many theories being circulated about the side effects for anyone made to undergo FGM, expecting any positive outcome may be a little cumbersome. The truth is that of the many countries and communities around the world that are now endowed with this system and practicing this ideology, none seem to be willing to freely give up the practice without a fight.

The question then arises as to why there always seems to be an obstacle every time concerns relating to giving up the practice are brought up. Could it be the male ego or the insecurity among women who have been made to believe that being a lady is not complete without marriage?

The following article and stories may further buttress the subject matter by bringing in a deeper understanding of the entire picture or the bottom-line.

A Dateline Health—Africa News Service article in 2003 by a staff reporter titled "Genital Cutting Does Not Eliminate Women's Sexual Sensation—Study" noted that Nigerian women who have undergone female genital cutting have been known to have the same propensity in regard to achieving sexual orgasm during sexual intercourse as those who have not been made to experience the exercise while engaging in the same practice, according to a study conducted in Edo State, Southwestern Nigeria, between 1998 and 1999.

According to the study group led by Dr. Okonofua, gynecologist and obstetrician, this important finding "negates the argument of female genital cutting proponents that cut women experience reduced sexual sensation (which is expected to make them less likely than uncut women to become sexually promiscuous)."

The study sample comprised 1,836 women, most of whom were married. The women were recruited at rural and urban antenatal and family planning clinics in a community where approximately 45 percent of the female population has undergone female genital cutting, usually in infancy. A structured questionnaire, administered by a trained nurse or midwife, was used to obtain data on socio demographic characteristics, sexual activity, and clinical history. A physician examined the women to determine the type of circumcision, if any, that the women had undergone.

Some 55 percent of participants had not undergone female genital cutting; 32 percent had undergone type I genital cutting (at least partial removal of the clitoris); 11 percent had undergone type II (at least partial removal of the clitoris and labia minora); and fewer than 2 percent had undergone type III (at least partial removal of the external genitalia and stitching or narrowing of the vaginal opening) or type IV (any other genital cutting).

In response to questions about sexual behavior, the study found that women who had undergone genital cutting were just as likely as those who had not to report having had recent sexual intercourse and were more likely to report at least sometimes initiating sexual intercourse with their partners. In addition, women who had been cut were at least as likely as uncut women to report regularly having an orgasm during sexual intercourse. Cut women were, however, less likely than uncut women to cite the clitoris and more likely to identify the breast as their most sensitive body part. This finding, according to the authors, "suggests that genital cutting does not eliminate a woman's sexual sensation, but instead shift(s) the point of maximal sexual stimulation from the clitoris or labia to the breast."

An East African female hunter

Some other significant observations emanating from the study were that cut women were significantly more likely than uncut women to report yellowish and bad-smelling vaginal discharge (odds ratio 2.8), white vaginal discharge (odds ratio 1.7), and lower abdominal pain (odds ratio 1.5). Though the reasons for the latter may not be well understood or inconclusive, the fact still remains that FGM is to date still practiced all over the world but known to be very common in developing countries as in Sub-Saharan Africa.

Though the preceding study may have concluded that side effects seen in women with cut genitalia appear to be not very different from those of their counterparts who have not gone under the knife, there are always exceptions in everything, which made the following stories very relevant in regard to the subject matter.

Peter, who is a Nigerian, had journeyed to the United States with his wife, Bose. She was a lucky selection from many of Peter's girlfriends because she had always wanted to travel abroad. Peter, who hailed from the Riverine area of the country where genital cutting is practiced, decided to take Bose with him. Since they were not married, there was a fast wedding ceremony quickly put together to join Peter and his cut friend together before they traveled to the United States. For some reason, Peter seemed to be complaining of his wife's indifferent feelings during sexual intercourse. But despite this concern, they had four children who were in elementary school when Bose decided that she would rather be alone since sex had never been fun to her. Her issue was the fact that she was terribly cut to the point of experiencing no feeling when having sex. The latter sounds like a rare occurrence, as I have not come across any other woman who was cut with such a story.

The second story is that of Juliet, who is now over fifty years old. During an interview on the subject, she noted that her urge for sex may have been diminished, but she continued enjoying sex to date with orgasms upon orgasms during sexual intercourse. The latter may be a variance from normal societal expectation, but it still shows that being cut does not necessarily mean that your sex drive is affected.

Chapter

7

Intended Control by Governmental Agencies around the Globe and Consequences

onsidering all the global attention being given to the subject of FGM, the need to completely eradicate the practice by every possible means or at least diminish this concern through all possible mediums of communication is more urgent. Governmental agencies around the world appear to have been coining possible rules, regulations, and stiff penalties for those communities and individuals found to be bent on continuing this heinous practice.According to Google, currently, there is anti-FGM legislation in only twenty-eight states in U.S., with twenty-two states for some reason still hesitant to protect girls from FGM by criminalizing it. Stephanie Chang, state legislator in Michigan's House of Representatives, on the Aha Foundation website noted that the legislation (against FGM) was bipartisan because representatives on both sides of the aisle were shocked by the fact that female genital mutilation was taking place in Michigan. As we learned more about what happened, we all understood how important it was to address this human rights issue immediately. We achieved bipartisan support for the bills through numerous conversations to ensure that we carefully vetted all the details of the bills and through talking to fellow legislators about the issue.

Senator Jane Nelson from Texas stated,

When I heard Ayaan Hirsi Ali talking to Tucker Carleton on Fox News about the case in Michigan, I was so horrified that I immediately reviewed our existing state laws to determine whether this could happen in Texas. While we had laws against the practice of FGM, we did not have anything in law to punish those who help facilitate the FGM practice by transporting girls to undergo this gruesome act. I introduced legislation. Every woman in the Texas Senate signed on as a joint author, and we overwhelmingly approved a new law making it a felony to transport girls for FGM procedures. I am so grateful for Ms. Hirsi Ali for courageously speaking out about this important issue. There is no place in our society for this barbaric practice.

Although FGM has been seen to be most common in immigrant communities and in major metropolitan areas of the United States, the data on this issue was first collected in 1990 with the use of census information. However, the CDC has reported a decrease in FGM in early 2010–2013, and Americans are blaming the growing levels of immigration for the number becoming higher. For some reason, FGM in most of the nineteenth and twentieth centuries was considered a standard medical procedure in the United States as a result of its prevalence in immigrant communities because physicians have been known to perform surgeries of varying invasiveness to treat a number of diagnoses, including hysteria, depression, nymphomania, and frigidity. As a result of the latter, FGM was allowed in the United States until the end of the twentieth century with some procedures covered by Blue Cross Blue Shield insurance until 1977.

It was not until 1996 that the federal law ban, titled the Genital Mutilation Act, passed to make it a felony for anyone found performing the gruesome act on anyone under the age of eighteen. For some reason, the act was stuck down as unconstitutional in 2018 by US federal district judge Bernard A. Friedman in Michigan, based on the argument challenging the federal government's authority to enact legislation outside the "Interstate Commerce" clause. As part of the ruling, Friedman also ordered that charges be dropped against eight people who had mutilated the genitals of nine girls.

It is known that in 2019, twenty-eight US states have made specific laws that prohibit FGM, with twenty-two states without specific laws against FGM. However, the United States has participated in several UN resolutions advocating for the eradication of FGM, including the UN's 1948 Universal Declaration of Human Rights, 1989 Convention on the Rights of the Child, and the Convention on the Elimination of All Forms of Discrimination against Women (CEDAW).

The United States is not the only country making laws to either eradicate the practice of FGM or diminish it as much as possible. Nigeria, in West Africa, has also followed suit. B. Eluaka (2003) of the Federal Ministry of Health, during a presentation on the National Policy on FGM and Plan of Action on the Elimination of Female Genital Mutilation in the Federal Capital Territory, Abuja, announced the approval of a National Policy and Plan of Action on the Elimination of Female Genital Mutilation (FGM) in Nigeria by the Federal Government of Nigeria. The document seeks "to reduce the proportion of girls and women who are at risk of undergoing any type of genital mutilation with a view to its eventual elimination."

The occasion of the public presentation was also used to inaugurate a coalition of nongovernmental organizations (NGOs) working on the elimination of FGM in Nigeria. Thirteen NGOs from ten states of the federation attended.

Female genital mutilation, commonly known as female circumcision, is practiced in practically every state in Nigeria, though in varying magnitude, from infancy to adulthood. The national prevalence rate is 40.5 percent. Prevalence at the state level, however, varies, ranging from 0.1 percent in Yobe State (northeast zone) to 98 percent in Osun State (southwest zone).

The document, approved by the Federal Executive Council on April 30, 2003, seeks to eliminate FGM, regarded as a violation of the human rights of women and girls. Four types of mutilation are practiced in Nigeria, with type 1 (excision of the prepuce with or without removal of part of or the entire clitoris) being the most prevalent.

Another contributor at the occasion was M. Amaeshi, Director of Community Development and Population Activities in the Federal Ministry of Health, who represented the minister of health, who lamented that despite various initiatives and efforts toward the elimination of FGM, the practice has continued to thrive, a situation he ascribed to its continued attachment to culture and tradition as well as ignorance.

Dr. Amaeshi urged all those at the ceremony to join in the crusade against all harmful traditional practices that were deeply rooted in our society, causing great havoc on our women and girls. According to him, "It is my hope that the practice (FGM) will be eradicated for a better tomorrow, good health and development for our women and girls."

A Senior Program Officer with the Inter-African Committee (IAC) on Harmful Traditional Practices, Mrs. Funso Orenuga, made a presentation on FGM, elaborating on its types, the myths, the consequences, and efforts carried out for its elimination. IAC has been in the forefront of fighting for the elimination of harmful traditional practices that target women and children in Africa.

The immediate health complications of FGM include pain, bleeding, shock, acute urine retention, and risk of blood-borne diseases, such as hepatitis B and HIV/AIDS. Long-term complications include recurrent urinary tract infections, dysmenorrhea, sexual dysfunction, chronic pelvic infection, infertility, prolonged and obstructed labor, vesico-vaginal fistulae (VVF), and recto-vaginal fistulae (RVF).

The occasion was also used to present another document, *Best Practices on the Elimination of Female Genital Mutilation: The Nigerian Experience*. The publication is a compendium of best practices that have been found most effective in the struggle to eliminate FGM, including activities involved and processes and strategies employed as well as success stories recorded.

Efforts to eliminate FGM are gradually yielding results in Nigeria. Ten of the thirty-six states of the country have legislated against it. The lower House of the National Assembly has also passed the bill while the Upper House is currently discussing it. Many previous circumcisers have given up the trade and have taken up alternative employment opportunities, while various interest groups are speaking out vocally against the practice, which is said not to have a single benefit.

In his remarks at the event, Dr. Abdoulie Jack, Acting WHO Representative in Nigeria, congratulated the government and people of Nigeria for the successful formulation and adoption of the National Policy and Plan of Action.

Recounting the strategic actions of WHO aimed at accelerating the elimination of FGM, especially in the African region, Dr. Jack said the WHO Nigeria office, since 1995, in active collaboration with other members of the UNDS, had worked closely with the National Technical Working Group on Harmful Traditional Practices to implement activities aimed at eliminating FGM.

He said he hoped that the implementation of the policy and plan would be effectively monitored while the national legislation, which gives full backing to the policy, would be passed soon.

The occasion featured cutting of a cake by children and adults present, in what was tagged "Celebrating victory for womanhood."

The occasion was also used to develop state work plans on elimination of FGM by the directors of Primary Health Care and Women-in-Health coordinators from the various states who were present. Also in attendance at the event were representatives of the media and international and bilateral agencies as well as NGOs or the nonprofit organizations.

An opinion page in the Nigerian newspaper *VanguardDaily* (Lagos) by Nowa Omoigui (2001) titled "HB22 Bill and Genital Mutilation" and subtitled, "For the National Assembly to Legislate on Female Circumcision Is to Criminalize Our Custom," Omoigui, who is also a medical doctor in South Carolina, USA expressed his unequivocal non support for the proposed HB22 Bill by Janet Adeyemi which is aimed at outlawing "Female Genital Mutilation Practice in the Federal Republic of Nigeria."

Expounding on the entire notion of FGM, the Doctor sees as a serious mistake in people not to understand that there is a "huge difference between Circumcision and Mutilation. To group all forms of age-old religious circumcision into one large category under the guise of medical enlightenment and "civilization" is very unfortunate". He believes that knowing of the "mischievous and hypocritical" nature of FGM, activists should be focusing on campaigning to ban "Male Genital Mutilation" instead. Dr. Omoigui opined that such movement would have joined the group of the much sophisticated gentile physicians [*not all gentile – Dr. Paul Fleiss is a prominent Jewish member*] led by Dr. George C. Denniston in the US who want male circumcision banned too [Doctors Opposing Circumcision (D.O.C.)]. Let us see who will sponsor that bill in Nigeria—to ban male circumcision—the main indication for which is cultural preference. [In other words, "We don't know why we do it."]

The classification system of types I, II, III, and IV being used for "female genital mutilation" is the same as was used in the US Congress when Pat Schroeder was sponsoring that country's bill. It is not true that every type of genital ritual has the same implication or is practiced consistently across Nigeria or Africa. I am not aware of any Edo woman—for example—who has been properly circumcised whose clitoris or labium was amputated. What is removed is the prepuce—a small piece of the sheath that extends from the clitoris. That sheath has no sexual function. [There is no evidence for this claim.] It is the same sheath that is removed in males. In fact in many cases the "removal" is symbolic—and is part of a traditional marriage ceremony.

Our Constitution recognizes religious secularity as a principle of state policy—but accepts Common law, Islamic law and customary law as a reality. It must be tolerant and also respect cultural secularity in a multicultural nation. There are ethnic clans in Nigeria—like Ijebus in the West and Itsekiris in the Mid-west—that do not routinely circumcise their women. [Women may notice this wording that defines them out of their clans and into the category of property.] I respect their right to exercise that prerogative and expect them to respect mine too.

Furthermore, there is absolutely no evidence that maternal and child mortality in Nigeria is increased because of properly performed circumcision. [Confining mortality to "properly performed" FGM defines it out of existence.] I challenge anyone to come out with randomized data that even remotely proves such a cause and effect relationship. [If this hasn't been studied, it certainly should be.] This is only the latest of a series of frivolous rationalizations that have been offered.

First the Women's liberation movement in the West said it was a male custom done to "control" women.

Then they discovered that female circumcision was done for women by women to women. [This is a common phenomenon— "slaves come to love their chains."] Next they said it limited sexual enjoyment—a fundamental right. But it is evident that most women who do not enjoy sex are not even circumcised. The latter may have been statistically true but trivial, because most women are not circumcised. The author contended. But to support his claim, Dr.

Omoigui would have to show that the proportion of cut women who do not enjoy sex is no greater than the proportion of intact women who do not. There are numerous reasons why a woman may not enjoy sex—including the competence of her male partner. Many post-menopausal women suffer such problems. Pessaries widely used for reasons other than circumcision cause plenty of genital damage to women in Nigeria and Africa (including gynaetresia)—but I haven't seen any legislation to ban use of pessaries. [Irrelevant. Demonstrating that there are other causes of sexual dysfunction says nothing about this one.] Now maternal and child mortality is being blamed on circumcision. It is just another case of intellectual fraud.

Is this not the same Nigeria where the government sanctions cutting of hands (i.e. mutilation of the limbs) based on religious codes of law in certain states? As civilized and advanced as the US is, one of their closest foreign allies is Saudi Arabia—a country where cutting of limbs and heads is standard operating procedure. Why are US organizations not leading the charge against the inimical health effects of amputation? Is oil greater than human rights? [Good questions, but irrelevant to FGM.]

Who advised the World Health Organization to coin the phrase "mutilation"? Whoever did was cynically manipulating language. We "mutilate" the umbilical cord by cutting it off at birth and arbitrarily deciding how long the navel should be. We "mutilate" our bodies with ear rings, tongue rings, tattoos, nose jobs etc. We "keep" biologically excretory products like nails and hair—and use them for beautification—and do so differently, I might add, depending on the cultural environment. Some western women (in the US) begin to shave their leg hair at age 10. Has anyone else in the world attacked them for mutilating what God put there for a reason? We use traditional marks for medicinal and symbolic.

Rather than "abortion" or "termination of pregnancy"—as my colleagues like to say—let us call it "fetal mutilation" (FM). Many of the so called advocates against circumcision who cry out against the loss of a small piece of tissue—and call it mutilation—have no qualms with the "right" to have abortions involving the barbaric crushing and scooping of body parts of an unborn fetus. Neither do I hear a worldwide campaign against episiotomy—the slashing (nor shall I say mutilation) of a woman's perineum to widen the passage for child birth—sometimes necessary, but more often not. The scar is permanent and the functional characteristics of the vault as a sexual organ may be altered forever.

Since we were children, how many doctors and women have we seen (or heard) charged to court for abortion in Nigeria—as unhealthy as it can turn out to be and as dangerous as it could be whether in the hands of quacks or specialists? And many women have become infertile or even died from sepsis. But it rides on in broad daylight while we are worrying about circumcision. How many Nigerian Gynecologists—including those who propound safe motherhood in public—can look you straight in the eye and say they have not been making money from D & Cs including partial birth abortions (i.e. fetal mutilation)?[Another argument by the name "Let's talk about something else." The issues in abortion and GM are different, and there are activists on both sides of the abortion debate.]

The cultural war against female circumcision is led by the same western human rights crowd that classifies same-sex marriages as okay (in some parts of the US), and puts pictures (of same sex couples) in books for little children to read and learn from. I have the right to invoke my ancient customs and look askance at such a policy—and protect my kids from it—at the risk of being called conservative. Even the Pope in his wisdom, saw it fit to apologize to traditional African religions recently for the value judgments that led to the destruction of their systems.

If inimical health outcomes of female circumcision are the concern of those who oppose it, let them tell us how to make it safer—just as male circumcision these days is often accomplished using a special device.

The number of neonates with neonatal tetanus from unhygienic cutting of cords in Nigeria has generally been addressed by measures to prevent tetanus—not to ban cord cutting. This point highlights one of the biases in female circumcision discussions—the fact that female circumcision was never taught to "modern" Nigerian doctors and not offered in hospital when a child is born. Therefore, the alleged relative safety and low risk of complications that attends male circumcision performed by trained physicians (not to mention the new technology for doing it) creates an unfair yardstick for comparison. And many of the best original experts in the villages are dying. Only recently, I accidentally discovered circumcisions—from an old villager.

What the Health Ministries in Nigeria should be doing in respectful consultation with traditional leaders—is restricting themselves to improving the safe performance of circumcision, or conducting randomized controlled studies to evaluate various traditional approaches to the matter, not dabbling into making jaundiced value judgments (through an arbitrary western prism) about an ancient blood ritual. That decision is for villages and clans to make, not the country as a whole.

An African mother with her child strapped on her back

Our children do not speak our language, do not wear our clothes, do not practice our religion, and our ancient customs are under assault. In 50–100 years we will be unrecognizable as a distinct cultural entity—all under the guise of globalization. Is this beneficial? To who? This rush to western judgment will have to be slowed down at some point.

> [*This is a serious consideration, and ending unhealthy, dangerous, and human-rights abusive customs like FGM and MGM should be done sensitively, "in consultation with traditional leaders," substituting customs that serve the same cultural function, without those harmful effects.*]

In conclusion, Dr. Omoigui stated that "criminalizing our customs is as dangerous and unwise as the analgesic effects of snail juice—used during undertaking". The National Assembly should stay out of legislating.

In a swift move, A. Raufu (2001), Lagos, Nigeria, in an article titled "Nigeria Recommends Jail Terms to Eradicate Female Genital Mutilation," noted that the Nigerian legislature is set to pass a law banning female genital mutilation and imposing a two-year jail term for offenders.

The bill, which is currently being considered by the Senate, was unanimously passed by Nigeria's lower house, the House of Representatives, last year. The Senate is expected to conclude its deliberations on the bill in May, after which it will be sent to President Olusegun Obasanjo for his assent.

The first clause of the Circumcision of Girls and Women (Prohibition) Bill says, "No person shall circumcise a girl or woman and no person shall abet or aid the circumcision of any girl or woman."

Already, some activists have complained that the two-year imprisonment prescribed by the new law is not strict enough, especially because it allows for an option of a fine of $100 (£69; €111) or the imposition of both a fine and incarceration. Some observers say, however, that the new law is a long-sought victory in the crusade to abolish female genital mutilation in Nigeria.

According to the bill, "circumcision of a girl or woman means cutting off all or part of the external sex organs of a girl or woman other than on medical grounds."

The law against female genital mutilation has been operational in five southern states out of the thirty-six states in Nigeria, and this will be the first nationwide law on female genital mutilation.

Female genital mutilation is a traditional practice in many parts of Nigeria, and it is regarded as an initiation rite that every girl must undergo before marriage. Elderly traditional practitioners, who often have neither medical training nor formal knowledge about anatomy, carry it out, and severe complications have occurred to women who undergo circumcision.

One reason that the practice has endured for so long among Nigerians, despite its obvious danger, is the notion that uncircumcised girls tend to be promiscuous. In many parts of Nigeria, girls who are uncircumcised are regarded as likely to have an unbridled appetite for sex, and some men will refuse to marry such women, particularly in Nigeria's rural communities. But Mrs. Atinuke Ige, a retired judge and critic of the practice, rejects this belief. "It is not true," she says. "I don't know what they mean by promiscuity. Every individual, male or female, is a product of what the home looks like. I think it is high time we stopped these abuses in the overall interest of the survival of Nigerian women."

Dr. Bene Madunagu, national coordinator of the Girls' Power Initiative, said,

> *Some of the negative effects of female genital mutilation include life threatening blood loss from circumcision, infection from unsterilized equipment, infertility, and injury to other organs and glands arising*

+

from a struggle by the victim during circumcision. Other effects are painful intercourse due to scar tissue blocking the vagina and labor complications from excessive scar tissue.

Al Jazeera contributors, Naib and Essa 2018 on Jaha Dukureh: "Don't Sensationalize FGM Survivors" focusing on Gambia in West Africa noted that 75 percent of girls in the country are subjected to FGM; with 30 percent of these young girls marrying before they turn 18. At the age of 15, Jana Dukureh was reportedly forced into marriage, after surviving the torture of female genital mutilation (FGM) when she was only a week old. Ironically, she was sent to New York to join her husband. The abuse did not stop here. The authors added that "On her wedding night, she was cut again to allow for the consummation of the marriage. The second procedure is common for women who have already undergone the most severe form of FGM."

Since living in the U.S. Dukureh's involvement as an activist against FGM was reported to have influenced former President Barack Obama in conducting more research relating to the abuse. The Al Jazeera contributors attributed Dukure, who is now a UN Goodwill Ambassador against FGM and the head of Safe Hands for Girls, an NGO supporting survivors in Africa efforts in her campaign in Gambia where she resides today as being responsible for the Gambian former President Yahya Jammeh's outlawing FGM in The Gambia in 2015. Jameh also attached penalties of $1,050.00 or three years imprisonment or both to the sentence. According to Naib and Essa, the former president's removal from office has since led to the resurgence of the practice. Lately, the fear of the spread of

HIV infection from unsterilized knives and other instruments has also helped to fuel the crusade against female genital mutilation.

A mother looking into the future expecting
possible solutions to this terrible practice

The story out of Dakar, Senegal, by Al Jazeera's Davinder Kumar (2013) in "Fighting Female Genital Mutilation in Africa" seemed to be of mixed connotations depending on your side of the issue. A Malian, whose name is Madina Bocoum Daff, described her experience when she was barely an adolescent as that of possibly ignorance by her family attempting to observe what had been laid down as a cultural part within her ethnicity from the Fulani community in Mali. The process involved "cutting" a girl's vagina enough to create what is described as a seal whose opening is narrow enough to enable the passing of urine and blood during menstruation. According to Kumar, Medina stated that "All I know is that I had severe problems immediately after being excised. I remember going through a very agonizing cycle of puberty. I remained covered in pain and humiliation." As horrifying and disturbing as Medina's narrative may sound, another Malian, Abdul, a father of two girls, literally said with dispatch, "I don't see any harm from this practice. It has been our tradition for centuries."

The death of thirteen-year-old Soheir al-Batea at the hands of a medical doctor while performing the procedure in a clinic in Egypt a few years back should be enough to show the proponents of FGM that there is no safe haven for exercising this procedure. The young girl's death, according to Al Jazeera, caused uproar and uncertainty all around a country where FGM is supposedly illegal but still widely practiced with more than two-thirds of the young women there being subjected to its barbaric nature.

Another thirteen-year-old, whose first name is Ahlam but whose family name, according to Kumar, had to be withheld for the sake of anonymity, describing her own ordeal, stated,

> *Immediately an old woman entered the room and got a razor out of her bag. My mother held my arms very tight so that I could not move. The woman used her razor to circumcise me. I cried loudly but nobody listened. The pain was unbearable. After all was done, my mom paid her some money and she left. A few hours later, I started to bleed.*

In the case of eleven-year-old Mariama, she could not separate herself from the never-ending thoughts that it would someday be her turn to be circumcised. This fear that seemed to be very present within her family was the reason they relocated to the capital of Bamako from the northern part of Mali, where the practice was so prevalent, especially after some natives were privy to witnessing the death of a friend's sister after her excision.

World Health Organization's Position on FGM

The World Health Organization on its website on FGM estimates that, globally, around 130 million women have been circumcised, with the highest incidence found in parts of Africa. In Western Nigeria alone, 89 to 90 percent of women have been circumcised.

According to the WHO website, FGM is classified into four major types:

- Type I—This is known as clitoridectomy, which means a partial or total removal of the clitoris. This procedure in some cases is done to remove only the prepuce, which is the skin surrounding the clitoris.

- Type II—This procedure is known as excision, meaning the partial or total removal of the clitoris and the labia minora, which are the inner folds of the vulva.

- Type III—This is called infibulation, which is the narrowing of the vaginal opening by creating a covering seal. This procedure is done through the formation of the seal by cutting and repositioning the labia minora or labia majora, sometimes through stitching with or without removing the clitoris.

- Type IV—This procedure is considered the most harmful to the female genitalia for nonmedical purposes, as it may involve pricking, piercing, incising, scraping, and cauterizing of the genital area.

Circumcision is often performed in unhygienic conditions. The majority of FGM takes the form of a clitoridectomy, which involves removing all or part of the clitoris. This is frequently performed by untrained people using blunt, unhygienic instruments, without anesthetic, often resulting in heavy bleeding, infections, and sometimes death. While considered by some cultures as an essential rite of passage to womanhood, opposition to the practice has largely come from outside these communities, with the United Nations pledging to eradicate it within three generations.

Another WHO report stated 100 to 140 million women have had vaginal mutilation around the world. Going by reports among the countries observing this tradition, the practice of FGM has led to the increase of prostitution among women who may have refused to go through this so-called "traditional rite."

WHO generally does not seem to see any health benefit whatsoever in this concept but only harm, as the risk does not seem to diminish considering the severity of the procedure. More so, most known victims are young girls, and only occasionally are adult women involved. WHO reported that more than three million girls are estimated to be at risk of being cut annually. This concern has, in some countries, led to trans ethnic and cultural intermarriages in these communities, resulting in destroying homes and in some cases causing strained relationships between families.

However, there is a sharp deviation from the initial WHO position on the health benefits attached to this practice because some studies have been known to show a lower risk of vaginal cancer, fewer infections from microbes gathering under the hood of the clitoris, and protection against herpes and genital ulcers. These studies by Western scientists have also shown a negative correlation between circumcision and HIV (August 15, 2017).

WHO, in conjunction with UNICEF and the United Nations Population Fund (UNFPA), had been working together for decades before the issuance of a joint statement in 1997 against the practice of FGM. If the exercise is to be successful, practicing communities have to decide to totally abandon the practice. The latter led to the 2007 initiation by UNFPA and UNICEF of a Joint Program on Female Genital Mutilation/Cutting to accelerate the abandonment process. In support of the latter, WHO, along with nine UN partners in 2008, issued a statement to eliminate the practice of FGM as they joined the increased advocacy for total abandonment, called "Eliminating Female Genital Mutilation: An Interagency Statement." In 2010, WHO, alongside other UN agencies and international organizations, published a "Global Strategy to Stop Health-Care Providers from

Performing Female Genital Mutilation." In spite of the passage by the World Health Assembly of Resolution WHA61 on elimination of FGM in 2008, it was not until December of 2012 that the UN General Assembly finally adopted a resolution on the elimination of female genital mutilation.

A 2017 Al Jazeera article titled "London Assembly Urges Mayor to Lead Campaign on FGM" reports that half of the FGM cases in the United Kingdom are in the city of London, with 65,000 girls reportedly at risk across the country. The London Assembly was reported to have called on Mayor Sadiq Khan to spearhead the campaign to end what is described as "the hidden crime" of FGM in the United Kingdom's capital. The report noted that an estimated 170,000 women and girls in Britain are known to have undergone FGM, and 65,000 preteen girls are believed to be at risk of being victims. As popular as the awareness against this concern is in the United Kingdom, one would expect some sort of reduction in the practice in the communities, but, for some reason, the contrary has been the case. Today, efforts to diminish this practice have resulted in health workers and teachers being required to report cases of FGM among the under-eighteen-year-old country-wide population. As much as Britain seemed to have strengthened the law on FGM, which was reportedly outlawed in 1985, there has never been any successful prosecution reported to date. However, it is believed that the London Assembly's focus is emphasizing its prevention and supporting those at risk rather than pursuing prosecutions.

Though the London mayor has not made any comment on if he would actually lead a campaign against FGM, it was reported that the mayor's deputy for policing, Sophie Linden, expressed her commitment to tackling what she described as an "appalling practice" (Reuter's News Agency).

In a subsection of *Sexual Mutilations: A Human Tragedy* (1997) titled "Redefining the Sacred" by Miriam Pollack, the author sees circumcision in males and females as a relic from the past. She noted that "even though female genital mutilation is far more destructive than male forced foreskin amputation, the issue cannot be reduced to one of competitive suffering." Pollack believed that challenging this concept or tradition may be likened to going head-on with the ancient notion of what is considered sacred. The author also embraced the notion of likening circumcision in general to pain. As relevant as the latter may sound, it still does not take away from the concept of culture, which is a learned behavior that later becomes the norm as the years and generations pass on. As noble as her position on pain may be, the importance of embracing the diverse cultures around the globe cannot be ignored. If the entire universe were to live by only certain rules embraced by some and rejected by others, being on the same page on all issues may be difficult to achieve. The fact that we all coexist is why we must learn and respect one another's beliefs regardless of how great or hash they may be.

However, opponents of FGM fear that the campaign against male genital mutilation (MGM) will distract attention from their campaign and that drawing parallels will weaken and trivialize the case against FGM. The Pollack article, using many familiar arguments to defend FGM, shows that our two human-rights struggles are basically the same.

M. Pollack (1996) in "Redefining the Sacred," a presentation at the Fourth International Symposium on Sexual Mutilations, University of Lausanne, Switzerland, addressed the issue of circumcision as involving both male and female, which she described as a practice done by our ancestors. Though the author saw more destruction being made to the female body than the male, whose circumcision she sees as a "foreskin amputation," most of the reports in support of the issue seem to see both in the same light. Pollack went further in her position on the issues as she described it as acknowledgment of the rights of our unborn babies and their bodies. The truth is the fact that circumcision is painful in the way and manner it is perpetrated be it on the man, woman, or baby.

However, some proponents for these concerns seem to beg to differ with Pollack's position and believe it is a tradition carried down generation after generation and will not succumb to some of the ways critics of the practice have continued to present the concerns to the universe—especially since most of them have never lived in the countries and communities engaged in the practice.

Chapter

9

Men's Involvement in Decisions Relating to FGM in Their Various Communities

Though WHO, UNICEF, the UN, and a host of other agencies may appear to be in favor of the total elimination of FGM from the universe, the truth still remains that eliminating cultures and customs that took a lifetime to build will always be impossible, if not close to it. Concerns that should be addressed now are those of enlightenment and education against FGM, stressing its disadvantages over its advantages and enabling the participating countries and communities around the world to relate to these concerns in a way that will bring the issues home and allow them to understand that FGM will affect the individuals' daily lives.

The motivation of FGM is based on the belief of what is considered acceptable sexual behavior and what is necessary in raising a girl and preparing her for adulthood and marriage. Moreover, since this issue is common in immigrant communities in the United States, FGM was considered a standard medical procedure in America for most of the nineteenth and twentieth centuries, with physicians performing surgeries of varying invasiveness to treat some medical diagnoses, which included hysteria, depression, nymphomania, and frigidity. With health insurance companies like Blue Cross Blue Shield covering this procedure until the end of twentieth century, it may have been seen as acceptable even in the United States, considering how everything is regulated in this part of the world.

Questions to be answered include the following: What do WHO, UNICEF, the UN, and other human rights agencies consider the politically correct way to handle the issue? What should be done that would be universally acceptable? Should the type of procedures practiced by physicians until the end of the twentieth century be considered the norm (especially when placed under close scrutiny)?

If a developed country like the United States is still out there searching for answers to stopping this inhumane practice, what can we say of developing and underdeveloped countries around the world, who seem not to be addressing the issue the way it needs to be addressed? Your guess is as good as mine. What is historically known is the unwillingness of the male individuals in the various countries and communities where FGM is being practiced to be involved in the decision-making process. This has been seen by some observers as some sort of control over these women by their male counterparts to possibly reduce their sexual urges while keeping themselves intact for their prospective husbands.

African leaders representing four generations pondering away out of the mess called FGM

The following story of a community leader, El Sheikh Saad, the father of a seven-year-old girl and the sheikh of his village mosque in Egypt's Assiut province can further illustrate the reason why every institution in the community should be involved in the all-out fight against FGM. The mosque leader had once been known not to be against the practice until he became educated on the health dangers. After he consulted with religious scholars, he decided to change his position on the issue. "I was not convinced about the harms of this tradition," he said. "I brought the matter up before the local religious committee, and they told me clearly that there was no religious basis for the practice."

The focus really should be the involvement of men in FGM-practicing countries in the decision-making to either reduce or eliminate this horrific practice. Since men are considered to be the head of the home in most countries around the world —even in developed countries, but only during tax-filing periods—it is of great importance for activism to be directed toward the male members of the perpetrating countries in order to reduce or eliminate the menace called FGM.

Girls and boys are not only rights holders themselves, but also future parents who will play a crucial role in ending this generational scourge.

—Madina Bocoum Daff, FGM survivor

References

Adinma, J. I. 1997. "Current Status of Female Circumcision among Nigerian Igbos." *West Afr. J. Med.* 16, no. 4 (October–December): 227–31.

Al Jazeera Social Media Community (2017)

Al Jazeera.com.

Breasted, James H. 1933. *The Dawn of Conscience*. New York: Scribner.

Bullough, V. 1976. *Sexual Variance in Society and History*. New York: Wiley Interscience.

Ehigiegba A. E., D. O. Selo-Ojeme, F. I. Omorogbe. *Female Circumcision and Determinants in Southern Nigeria.* Department of Obstetrics and Gynecology, University of Benin Teaching Hospital, Nigeria.

Everydayhealth.com.

Goodman, J. 1996. "Challenging Circumcision: A Jewish Perspective." Presented at the Fourth International Symposium on Sexual Mutilations, University of Lausanne, Lausanne, Switzerland.

Harris, James E. and Kent R. Weeks. 1973.*X-raying the Pharaohs.* New York: Scribner.

https://en.wikipedia.org/wiki/Female_genital_mutilation_in_the_United_States.

https://www.alternet.org/2019/05/trump-and-barr-wont-defend-ban-on-female-genital-mutilation/.

https://www.who.int/news-room/fact-sheets/detail/female-genital-mutilation.

Larue, Gerald. 1991. "Religious Traditions and Circumcision." Presented at theSecond International Symposium on Circumcision, San Francisco, CA, April 30–May 3, 1991. http://www.nocirc.org/symposia/second/larue.html.

Maimonides, Moses. 1963.*The Guide of the Perplexed, Vols. I & II.* Translated by Shlomo Pines. Chicago: University of Chicago Press.

Moss, L. 1991. "The Jewish Roots of Anti-Circumcision Arguments." Presented at The Second International Symposium on Circumcision, San Francisco, CA, April 30–May 3, 1991.http://www.nocirc.org/symposia/second/moss.html.

Odujinrin, O. M., C. O. Akitoye, M. A. Oyediran. 1989. "A Study on Female Circumcision in Nigeria." *West Afr. J. Med.* 8, no. 3 (July–September):183–92.

Ogunlola I. O., E. O. Orji, A. T. Owolabi. *Female Genital Mutilation and the Unborn Female Child in Southwest Nigeria.*Department of Obstetrics, Gynaecology and Perinatology, Obafemi Awolowo University Teaching Hospitals Complex, Ile-Ife, Nigeria.

Okonofua, F.E., et al. 2002. "The Association between Female Genital Cutting and Correlates of Sexual and Gynaecological Morbidity in Edo State, Nigeria." *British Journal of Obstetrics and Gynaecology*, 109, no. 10: 1089–1096.

Pollack, Miriam. 1997.*Sexual Mutilations: A Human Tragedy*. New York: Plenum Press.

Religioustolerance.org/fem_circ.htm.

Reuter's News Agency.

Omoigui, Nowa 2001. "Female Genital Mutilation Practice in the Federal Republic of Nigeria." Vanguard Newspapers, Lagos Nigeria

Theahafoundation.org.

Wilson, John. 1950 "Circumcision in Egypt." In *Ancient Near Eastern Texts Relating to the Old Testament,* edited by James F. Pritchard, 326. Princeton: Princeton University Press.

Cesca, Bob (*Salon*2019) On US Defense Against FGM

Webster's II New Riverside University Dictionary 1984, 1988 by Houghton Mufflin Company

Althaus, Frances 1997 'Female Circumcision: Rite of Passage Or Violation of Rights?' presented by during the 'International Family Planning Perspectives Volume 23, Number 3, September 1997

Hosken, Fran 1982. *"The Hosken Report: Genital and Sexual Mutilation of Females"* Reviewed by: Margaret Jean Hay *The International Journal of African Historical Studies.* Vol. 14 No. 3 (1981). Pp. 523-526. Published by: Boston University African Studies Center.

Wamai, R, Geisheker, J, Morris, B & Majome, J 2014 "Do the health benefits of male circumcision outweigh the risks" Associate Professor, Northeastern University; Executive Director, Doctors

Opposing Circumcision, Professor Emeritus, University of Sydney, Member of Parliament, Zimbabwe

Naib, F & Essa, A, 2017 "Why should we care about FGM?"

Naib, F & Essa, A, 2018 Jaha Dukureh: "Don't Sensationalize FGM Survivors"

doctorsopposingcircumcision.org

Jessie Majome @jessiefmajome

jessiefmajome.org.zw

www.en.wikipedia.org/wiki/List of HIV%2FAIDS cases and.

www.news-medical.net/health/HIV-andAIDS-Research.aspx.

www.who.int/gho/hiv/en/.

Printed in the United States
By Bookmasters